Circles of Love

Circles of Love

Stories of Congregations
Caring for People with Disabilities
and Their Families

*Dean Preheim-Bartel,
Timothy J. Burkholder,
Linda A. Christophel,
and Christine J. Guth*

 **Herald Press**

Harrisonburg, Virginia
Kitchener, Ontario

Library of Congress Cataloging-in-Publication Data

Preheim-Bartel, Dean A.

 Circles of love : stories of congregations caring for people with disabilities and their families / Dean A. Preheim-Bartel, Timothy J. Burkholder, Linda A. Christophel, and Christine J. Guth.

      pages cm

 Includes bibliographical references.

 ISBN 978-0-8361-9987-1 (pbk. : alk. paper) 1. Church work with people with disabilities. I. Title.

 BV4460.P73 2015

 259'.4--dc23

2015010642

This book is published in collaboration with the Anabaptist Disabilities Network (www.adnetonline.org). Two previous books sponsored by the Anabaptist Disabilities Network include *Supportive Care in the Congregation* and *After We're Gone*; see pages 89–90 for more information.

CIRCLES OF LOVE

© 2015 by Herald Press, Harrisonburg, Virginia 22802
      Released simultaneously in Canada by Herald Press,
      Kitchener, Ontario N2G 3R1. All rights reserved.
Library of Congress Control Number: 2015010642
International Standard Book Number: 978-0-8361-9987-1
Printed in United States of America
Design by Reuben Graham
Cover art by Chad Friesen

Photograph on page 59 by Roaming Reflections Photography, used with permission. Photograph on page 78 by Robert John Friesen, Fine Art Photographer, all rights reserved, used with permission. Other photographs courtesy of ADNet.

To order or request information, please call 1-800-245-7894, or visit www.heraldpress.com.

19 18 17 16 15   10 9 8 7 6 5 4 3 2 1

Contents

Foreword

by Bill Gaventa

I grew up as a Baptist missionary kid in Nigeria in the 1950s and early 1960s. I experienced wonderful hospitality in both the small and large churches our family visited. Often, in a small village in the "bush," we would be invited to an elder's home for refreshments after the service. It was amazing how often an iconic American product would show up in those refreshments as the most significant offering they could give us: a warm bottle of Coca-Cola. Cokes were there, even the advertisements. Refrigeration was not.

Nigerian families take their family ties very seriously, so much so that if a very distant relative shows up on your front doorstep, you are obliged to take them in. That strong sense of connection and obligation is sometimes oppressive, but it also lives out the African concept of *ubuntu*, which means, simply, "I am who I am through others."

Back in America in the twentieth century, as Dean A. Preheim-Bartel points out in his introduction, cultural values were changing as images of independence, mobility, and achievement often led to a loss of a sense of community or social network. These changes have led to increased stratification and a lack of what community builders call "third places": places beyond home and work where people from diverse backgrounds can get to know one another and form supportive communities where needs and gifts alike are shared.

The church, obviously, has incredible potential to be the most powerful "third place." As English lingo in Nigeria would say, "it is no small thing" that Paul's chapter on faith, hope, and love in 1 Corinthians is preceded by the metaphor of the church as the body of Christ. Every part is connected with the whole. Cultural values of importance and strength are turned upside down, so to speak. Everyone is a part of the body. If someone is separate from the body, for whatever reason, there is loss, not just to that person but also to the life and function of the whole.

A belief in faith, hope, and love in these times is not just living out our call; it is countercultural. This is especially the case for individuals or families who do not measure up to "normal" standards of success when judged by the values of our society. These people are often shunned, implicitly or explicitly, as if somehow it was their responsibility, their sin, or their lack of faith.

Thus a body of believers that steps in and says, in word and deed, that everyone is truly welcome and that we belong to one another in the body of Christ is making the most effective and authentic witness it can make. It is no wonder that many of the articles and research studies on the growing number of people who identify themselves as "nones" report that they avoid organized religion because they have been wounded by congregations who do not practice what they preach.

In this delightful and powerful short book, we find stories of congregations that have found ways to live out the biblical call to respond to one another's needs by using one another's gifts. These congregations, when presented with the needs of a person with a disability and/or their family, did not follow the example of the disciples by the sea when they suggested to Jesus that he respond to the hunger of five thousand people by referring them to other helping organizations or by looking for a large grant so they could do the feeding themselves. "No," he answered both times; "You do it." In the best of what we now call asset-based community building, he saw capacity and gifts where the disciples saw only scarcity and limits. All it took was a small boy to step forward and say, "I can help. Let me share what I have."

The common thread in all of these stories is a demonstration of what I sometimes call the "magic of church." Someone, a parent or pastor or layperson, first makes explicit an individual's need within the congregation, and people respond. They respond in different ways and out of the different gifts and skills they have, which is also part of the magic by which diversity shows its power and individual offerings are multiplied beyond expectation.

Then, second, others do not let their uncertainty overwhelm them. Essentially the church says, "We are not sure how to do this, but let us figure it out with you." Then a journey of trial and error leads to bonds of partnership and trust, respect for one another, and—the final piece of magic—everyone grows and is helped in the process. Givers become receivers. Receivers become givers. Expectations and patterns get turned upside down. The body of Christ grows stronger because of it.

A paradox of this kind of faith, hope, and love is that the internal work of the faith community, in making sure its members are connected and supported, becomes an external witness when the stories are told. That is the other power of this book. Dean and Al (Aldred Neufeldt) and others who worked on *Supportive Care in the Congregation* and its revised edition were outlining possibilities—a potential treatment plan, as it were. Or, to get away from a medical model, you could call it a person-centered, Christ-centered model of possibilities. Part of its effectiveness was that they did not say, "This is the only way to do it." Now Dean and his new coauthors follow up with these stories, which people will remember long after they forget theory and theology. These stories can be told and shared across faith networks and disability networks, and can empower because people can see, in real flesh, potential and possibility. Systems of care call them "natural supports." We might make an argument for "supernatural supports."

Another African proverb is a favorite of mine, one I learned as an adult back in the United States: "When there is a thorn in the foot, the whole body must stoop to pluck it out." In the stories in this book, the body is plucking out some of the thorns. More importantly, the body of Christ is helping others through briar patches. Walk with them, and let them challenge your soul . . . and body.

Bill Gaventa, MDiv
Director, Summer Institute on Theology and Disability
Director, Collaborative on Faith and Disability

Foreword

by Joe Landis

Reading *Circles of Love* brought to mind my great-uncle Jonas Alderfer. People said he had "the mind of a child" but that he loved to work. He spent his life living and working on different family farms. He outlived his parents and his sister and ended up living out his days with his nephew. He was baptized into Salford Mennonite Church, where he never missed a church function and contributed to the building fund from his miniscule savings. On Sunday mornings, he always sat on a front bench, turning around to scan the congregation and see who was there. This church congregation provided a community where Jonas was always at home.

Present-day faith communities are shaped by important biblical texts that call us to respond to the marginalized in our communities, including people with disabilities. This biblical call runs counter to the individualism of popular culture. Yet, motivated by compassion and the desire not to offend, church leaders often hesitate to approach persons with disabilities and their families to listen to their stories and respond to their needs. I call this the "hesitation blues." It matters not whether you come from a large or small congregation, a new, old, shrinking, or growing congregation; most suffer from the hesitation blues.

Families who have members with disabilities, for their part, are often so overwhelmed with the challenge of advocating for a loved one that they have little strength or initiative left to reach out to their faith community. They may believe, as parents have told me in the past, "Church is not a place to put yourself forward, burden others, or complain." And so, not out of disrespect or bad intention, the hesitation blues continue, and both parties go off in separate directions, as if vanishing into the Milky Way.

Circles of Love offers example after example of congregations that have overcome the hesitation blues and built on an understanding that we are all part of God's family. These congregations, like the one that welcomed my uncle Jonas, have learned that the biological family, while often promoted as the key unit of society, cannot carry this weight alone. Biological families die out. God actually calls us to be part of a bigger family: God's family.

When the apostle Paul mentions biological families, he offers this prayer:

> This, then, is what I pray, kneeling before the Father, from whom every family, whether spiritual or natural, takes its name: Out of his infinite glory, may he give you the power through his Spirit for your hidden self to grow strong, so that Christ may live in your hearts through faith, and then, planted in love and built on love, you will with all the saints have strength to grasp the breadth and the length, the height and the depth; until, knowing the love of Christ, which is beyond all knowledge, you are filled with the utter fullness of God. (Ephesians 3:14-17 JB)

This is the mystery at the heart of the stories in *Circles of Love*. How God builds his kingdom is a mystery, but if we listen to each other, we can do what we know is right and in this way we can go about transforming lives. While our focus may start with doing good for someone else, we find that our hidden selves flourish as well. Our congregations, and, in turn, the wider communities that surround them, become whole by engaging everyone's gifts. To borrow words from Gregory Boyle, "It's about God's own dream come true, that there be kinship."[1]

Joe Landis
CEO and founder, Peaceful Living

Preface

Christine J. Guth

The vision for this book captured my imagination following a conversation over coffee with Dean Preheim-Bartel in 2009. At the time, Paul Leichty and I, working together for Anabaptist Disabilities Network (ADNet), were intrigued by the persistent attention *Supportive Care in the Congregation* was receiving outside Mennonite circles. Twenty-five years after the book's first publication, we were often hearing disability advocates within various Christian denominations promote it. ADNet had become custodian of the remaining supplies of that small book when our organization formed to carry on the disability advocacy among Anabaptist churches that Mennonite Central Committee had begun decades earlier and that Mennonite Mutual Aid (now Everence) had continued until 2002.

Anticipating that *Supportive Care in the Congregation* would soon be out of print, Paul, as ADNet's executive director, began to explore the idea of updating and republishing it. This led us to talk with Dean Preheim-Bartel, one of the book's authors, to learn the history behind it and to solicit his support for the revision.

One part of the conversation that impressed me was hearing Dean's long-held hope for a sequel to *Supportive Care in the Congregation*, which would tell stories about congregations

15

that had put its model into practice. The idea of a book of supportive care stories caught my attention. The part of my role at ADNet I like best has been telling stories—stories that spark the imagination about what is possible for communities of faith who include people with disabilities as natural and valued members of the body of Christ. Stories have power to move hearts and inspire action. Stories might attract a wider readership and encourage others to try out the model and its theological vision as outlined in *Supportive Care in the Congregation*.

The vision of providing a congregational network of care for persons with significant disabilities was close to my heart because of personal and family experience. I knew firsthand both the isolation resulting from living with disability and the blessing of care from a group of sisters and brothers in Christ, walking with me and my family. As I wrote in my preface to the 2011 edition of *Supportive Care in the Congregation*, "An intentional network of Supportive Care that surrounds a family stuck in the mud of disability-related crises can be the strong arm that the family desperately needs. Such care embodies God's love for us where we need it most." The presence of God's love in tangible form during difficult times allowed my faith to survive much struggle. The support I received bore fruit, inspiring the work I now do for ADNet.

The idea of a book of supportive care stories took root and remained with me after we had successfully republished *Supportive Care in the Congregation*. It persisted while we tried to come up with a way that ADNet, with its limited resources, could move this idea forward and share the vision of supportive care more widely.

Through the efforts of our four authors and many others, *Circles of Love* is now a reality. We have widened the original vision to include stories from congregations that have used other practical models of support. We express deep appreciation to the individuals, families, and congregations who allowed us to include their stories in this book, and to others who shared stories we were not able to include.

We are grateful to Sue Cassel, who worked with me in the early stages to pursue potential story leads, develop interview questions, and collect initial information from many respondents. Thanks to ADNet's board of directors and many others who provided us with story possibilities. Thanks to photographer Robert Friesen and others who shared photos with us. We are grateful to the Fransen Family Foundation and the Schowalter Foundation for grants that helped make the writing and publishing possible. Thanks to Julie Diener, who allowed us to use *The Crowds Following Jesus*, one of Chad Friesen's paintings (see chapter 5), on the book cover.

The book has truly been a collaborative effort. Timothy Burkholder, first as executive director for ADNet and later as a volunteer, provided project management and drafted chapter 8. He also gets credit for recruiting Dean Preheim-Bartel and Linda Christophel to the project. Linda did most of the interviewing and encouraged us to expand the geographic and cultural diversity of the stories. From material collected by Sue Cassel, Linda, and me, Dean Preheim-Bartel drafted the chapters (except for chapter 8). My role included carrying the vision, searching for story leads, editing, and bringing together all the final details.

As followers of Jesus Christ, we continue his healing work when we embody his love to one another in both small and large ways. These stories provide us with specific glimpses into communities empowered by the Holy Spirit, growing together in grace, joy, and peace, with God's healing and hope flowing through them to the world.[2] May these stories spark your imaginations about what is possible in your congregations and provide you with inspiration to take action. May God's grace and blessing meet you on your journey.

Introduction

Dean A. Preheim-Bartel

As a boy growing up in central Kansas, I was aware that a prominent family in our church included an individual who was "different." Harold (not his real name) lived with his brother and family. Everyone in town knew him by name, and we would occasionally see him doing odd jobs for various storekeepers downtown. On warm summer afternoons, he often walked up and down Main Street or visited at the corner of Main and Grand Streets with other elderly gentlemen under the shade of a large maple tree.

On one such summer afternoon, Harold came across my father, who had fallen into a streetscape planter and could not get up. He helped my father, who had physical disabilities, out of the planter and walked him the three blocks to our house.

In those days, the village provided the necessary care and support for many of its residents with disabilities. In our rural community, there was no shame in having a brother with a disability; it just was. No structured programs existed for persons like Harold, but everyone in town looked out for him, just as he looked out for others.

Now, some sixty years later, it becomes necessary to write a book about the kinds of support churches can provide to those among us who experience disabilities or other life difficulties.

We can no longer assume that persons like Harold will receive the kind of support and attention they need from their community or from their church. It is important to build support structures into the life of our congregations.

For twenty-five years I advocated for and with persons with disabilities and their families in the community and in churches. I was witness to the strides made in our society, but also to the prejudice society had yet to overcome.

This book introduces individuals and families who have received support from caring people in congregations, support that has changed the course of their lives. These are not stories of valor or victory but of ordinary people whose lives have been transformed by circles of love in their own congregations.

In chapter 1 we meet a young man who simply dreamed of living independently, a dream realized because a group of people in his church dedicated themselves to showing him how to achieve his goal.

Chapter 2 recounts the story of a family touched by tragedy and loss who received the love and compassion of one small rural congregation. They experienced this love not only in time of crisis, but also over the long haul, holding the family together.

In chapter 3 we meet the Smith family, whose world turned upside down when son Ben changed from an engaging, happy child into a troubled young adult with a diagnosis of schizophrenia. We also become acquainted with their care network, who shared the Smiths' journey, lightened their load, and improved Ben's quality of life.

In chapter 4 we get to know Cindy, a mother who, through advocating for her children, became a leader pushing for change in her congregation. She spoke up for other parents when they were at their most vulnerable.

Chapter 5 tells the story of Chad and the vision of his congregation, Southside Fellowship. "The Business of Support" does not intend to show how to institutionalize support, but how a congregation's love for a young artist made it possible for him to share his art. Through his God-given gift of painting, he revealed the depths of his convictions, the joy in his heart, and the pain in his soul.

Waiting expectantly for their first child is the dream of most parents. In chapter 6 we meet Christine, who confronted a different reality. One of her twins experienced extensive medical problems, but her church poured out love and support for this new mother.

Parenting does not come with an instruction manual, especially when a child is on the autism spectrum. Chapter 7 recounts the story of a family who courageously shared their needs with their congregation. They found an understanding pastor and supportive congregation, ready and willing to respond.

Norma turned her pain into positive action by planning for a new congregational ministry called See Me. With the encouragement of her pastors, she has also completed Bible and leadership training to become the director of Christian education for all ages in her congregation. Read chapter 8 to learn about the significance of friendship in Norma's story.

Where would you turn if you needed an ever-increasing level of personal care? Would your church be up to the task of providing it? Deep commitments enable members of Reba Place Fellowship to step in with the care Bob needs. In chapter 9, you will learn about members of his household who feel called to care for Bob, and how this call has changed the life of one care partner.

Chapter 10 introduces additional churches that have chosen other approaches to provide compassionate care and unique support to those on the margins of our society and those dependent on others for their well-being.

This book has been twenty-nine years in the making. Ever since I coauthored *Supportive Care in the Congregation* in 1986, it has been my dream to publish stories of success from Anabaptist churches that have used the model outlined in the original book. As we began our research for this book, however, we discovered two things: The original book has received more attention from non-Anabaptist denominations than we expected; and Anabaptist churches have tended to see this model not as unique, but rather as "how we do church."

Several of the churches described in this book studied *Supportive Care in the Congregation* and followed the steps it outlines, but a majority did not. We recognize, however, that these congregations met significant family needs through informal support. In doing so, they illustrate key principles of the model.

I hope you will find this book inspiring and instructive as together we seek to minister to families with special needs.

1

Support for Independence

Belmont Mennonite Church and Kent Gunden

The oldest of five children, Kent Gunden took pride in being the older brother. His sister, Sher, was born thirteen months after Kent, and thirteen months later their brother Dennis was born. When Kent was about nine years old, his family moved from Illinois to Elkhart, Indiana. As a student with developmental disabilities, he entered a special needs class a few doors down from his sister's classroom. His younger sister recalls that Kent was her constant classmate because they shared the same grade level. He was always present at the same school functions. "I was always Kent's sister, his protector," she recalls. Kent's brother Dennis was a standout athlete. Kent became the team manager for many of his teams, and that kept Kent out of trouble with the athletes.

Sher was reserved, and Kent more outgoing. Sometimes she was embarrassed by his behavior. Going through school as Kent's younger sister was difficult. The emotional weight of being her brother's "protector" was heavy when peers were unaccepting of differences. Sher learned that she could not always protect Kent from embarrassing moments.

It was not lost on Kent that he was the oldest child in the family. He resented a younger brother or sister asking or telling him to do something. His siblings sometimes resented the fact that much of family life revolved around Kent and his needs. After a while, Sher learned that the more choices Kent had, the less he felt he was "being handled" and the more cooperative he became. When he felt respected for his thoughts and ideas, or just for being who he was, he became more agreeable.

When I (Dean Preheim-Bartel) first met Kent's mother, Evelyn Gunden, she was a single mother and a secretary in the office where I worked. Kent, at age twenty-eight, was living in a group home for adults with disabilities. He had lived there for ten years, but the restrictions of group living were increasingly confining for Kent and troubling to Evelyn. In an attempt to modify Kent's behavior, the staff had started requiring him to earn points to see his mother. One morning when Evelyn came in to work, she was especially frustrated. "Kent should be able to talk to his mother whenever he wants to!" she exclaimed. "What do you think I should do?"

At the time, I was serving as a disability consultant for an international church agency, Mennonite Central Committee, and Evelyn had become my administrative assistant. I realized that her concern for her son's situation provided the perfect opportunity for me to test a new family support model I was working on with another disability consultant. I described the model to Evelyn and asked, "Would you and your son be willing to try out this model with your church?" At first she had some concerns. She wanted Kent to be able to live more independently, but if he gave up his space in the group home, Evelyn knew they could expect a long wait for readmittance should he ever need to return. She also wondered if people in her church would be willing to make the time commitment this would require. Soon, however, she was ready to take the risk.

Evelyn recounted an earlier experience that Kent had had at their church, which reassured her that the church would respond positively:

I noted in our church bulletin one Sunday that during the month of September there would be weekly special music during worship. Members were invited to participate using musical instruments, which they would play along with the choir. Kent saw this announcement and asked if I thought he could play the tambourine for the group. I told him he should ask Stan, the music director. When Kent is interested enough to do something, he is very capable of following through. He approached Stan as soon as the last amen was uttered! Being the kind of person Stan is, he told Kent, "Certainly. We'd be glad to have you." I was sure Stan didn't know what he was in for, but I appreciated the spirit in which Kent was accepted.

When it came time to practice the following Saturday, Kent called Stan and asked him for a ride to church. Stan suggested that Kent stand out in the middle of the aisle in front of the choir to play the tambourine by himself for one verse. Knowing how much Kent likes the limelight, my prayers began that he wouldn't put on "some kind of show." I'd known for many years that Kent had natural rhythm. After all, he'd been pounding out rhythm on whatever was handy for twenty-some years, but never with a group or in a public program. Why couldn't I just relax, not worry about what kind of show he might put on? Why couldn't I just accept his excitement and desire to praise God in this way, the same as other members of the church would?

That Sunday morning, as the worship leader announced the special music, I could feel the tension throughout my body. I tried to relax, knowing people in our church are very accepting of Kent and would understand. I was hardly prepared for what happened. First, I noticed Kent looked a little hesitant— just like most persons during their debut—so I found myself saying a prayer, "Lord, help him to do his best." Then the piano began, and right on cue Kent began to play that tambourine in a way that I have never seen or heard before. I don't believe he missed a beat, and as I began to relax, I thoroughly enjoyed the rendition. Toward the end, I began to feel a new kind of worshipful experience. Kent played that tambourine in the most professional way, without any kind of show, and God was truly glorified.

I cannot find words to express the new joy I felt as Kent was allowed to praise God in a way that is so natural to him. One friend after church said to me with tears in his eyes, "My, that was a wonderful experience to see and hear Kent play this morning. I just wonder what else is locked up in that boy that we haven't allowed to come out." There were other expressions of appreciation for this experience, and again I thanked God for a church family that is accepting and open to all its members.[3]

Kent was an outgoing person. If overexuberant at times, he also had reasonably good interpersonal skills. He did not know a stranger; he talked to anyone. His hope was to live independently, but he would need considerable support and assistance to achieve that goal. The supportive care model I wanted to test would require buy-in from Kent and Evelyn and their congregation, Belmont Mennonite Church.

With Evelyn's permission, I approached her pastor, Duane Beck, about setting up a team from Belmont to support Kent in independent living. Pastor Beck was enthusiastic and found various church members to form a support group.

At the first meeting, I described the project and assured the volunteers that responsibilities related to Kent would be divided and shared. No one person would be given more responsibility than they were willing to carry. We thought this might be a key to the success of this model. Preparing Kent to live independently would require teaching him a variety of skills. The volunteers soon understood that as support group members, they could play a key role in helping Kent learn each of these skills.

As a testimony to God's guidance in this process, support group volunteers who had the necessary skills soon signed up to fill all the critical roles. One member agreed to help Kent manage his money; another would help him prepare menus and take him grocery shopping; a social worker agreed to help Kent understand how his actions affected others around him. Several members offered friendship by taking Kent out to lunch on a regular basis and to local high school sporting events, one of Kent's favorite activities.

A retired teacher in the support group wrote this insightful description of the group's purpose: "The Support Group is an attempt to help guide Kent, advise and affirm him, correct his course if he waivers, and provide transportation and social contacts as needed."[4] It was deeply reassuring to Evelyn that others cared enough about Kent to commit their time to him.

In time, the range of support from this care group enabled Kent to move from a highly structured group home to his own apartment. During this same time, Kent completed training to get his first paying job at a fast-food restaurant. With all the changes in Kent's life, the group set up a schedule for a family member or support group member to call Kent each evening. They talked with him about his day, celebrated his successes, and identified problems that needed attention. This continued for about a month. While the transition to greater independence had many bumps along the way, it was a risk well worth taking. The group walked with Kent through several different apartments, misspent monies, cooking fiascoes, and the theft of his bicycle.

During the first years, the supportive care team met monthly to coordinate care. The group's active support was integral to Kent's establishing himself in independent living. As patterns and relationships solidified, he needed less assistance, and team meetings became less frequent. After about ten years, the team disbanded. Kent and his family no longer needed this structure, but many of the relationships continued. Evelyn often said that the support group was also beneficial to her. Even years later, she felt comfortable calling members of the original group if she needed to.

Kent thrived on his independence. Eventually he moved up from a bicycle to his own motor scooter, managed a paper route for many years, and became relatively successful at living independently. He lived in a variety of apartments, earning a good recommendation from each property owner. When in his mid-fifties, Kent moved into the retirement community where his mother was living. This meant stable housing for him the rest of his life. Evelyn passed away on February 5, 2013. Kent's siblings now provide primary assistance and support to him as he continues to live in the retirement community and to be actively involved in his church.

Several years after the support group was formed, Evelyn and I agreed that our pilot project was functioning smoothly. By following our proposed guidelines within the model, the group successfully carried out its purpose and helped Kent achieve his goal. As a result, international human services consultant Aldred H. Neufeldt and I coauthored *Supportive Care in the Congregation*, detailing the model that Belmont had initiated so successfully. Mennonite Central Committee published the first edition of the book in 1986.[5]

I recently sat down with Kent to reflect, some thirty years later, on the value of the support group for him. He gave it positive marks, especially noting how important it had been in preparing him for greater independent living.

Kent Gunden in his present apartment.

During the time this support group was active, Belmont pastor Duane Beck attended a retreat for persons with disabilities and their families. He came away inspired and educated by these families. Based on what he had learned from them and on his own experience with Kent's support group, he shared the following suggestions for congregations wanting to support people with disabilities. They later appeared in the Mennonite

Disabilities Committee newsletter. Nearly thirty years later, they are still pertinent:

- Relating informally to persons with disabilities can make a big difference. Simple things like a smile, shaking hands, giving a hug, saying hello, making eye contact, using age-appropriate language, all help a person feel valued.
- Appropriately integrate persons with disabilities into all aspects of church life, such as Sunday school, worship, and fellowship, utilizing their interests and gifts. Making church buildings accessible is a welcoming act.
- Sit down with families and listen to their stories, wishes, and needs. They are just ordinary people with extraordinary needs. They love, care, and hurt just like the rest of us. They run out of energy and patience too. They need support from the congregation that will build up their faith, hope, and love. Leaders of the congregation are responsible to take the initiative and find out how the congregation can help, and then rally support. Don't leave all this work to the parents.
- Be open and sensitive to the blessings available to us from persons with disabilities if we open our hearts and observe and listen. They just may be ministers of God's grace to us.[6]

• • • • • • • • • • • •

It was rewarding to see our model of supportive care work effectively. As I evaluated the keys to the success of this model for Kent, several things stood out:

1. The full support of the pastor from the beginning facilitated the formation of the group.
2. Kent was already well known, established, and accepted in the congregation.

3. People in the congregation seemed more willing to participate when they realized their responsibilities would be limited to a single role that fit their own gifts. This is a central tenet of the model, because it reduces burnout and fosters greater collaboration and cooperation among support group members.

4. The tangible and realistic goal of moving Kent toward much greater independence was the clear driver of the support group's initial activities.

2

Long-Term Family Support

Olive Mennonite Church and the Larson Family

What can a church do to help when a family breadwinner dies unexpectedly? In 2004 Calvin Larson,[7] longtime member of Olive Mennonite Church, died suddenly of a heart attack. His survivors included his wife, Betty, and three children still living at home: twin daughters and a son. Betty had a variety of health problems, and teenage son Jay was born with developmental disabilities.

Initially, men from the rural church in Elkhart County, Indiana, jumped into action by cutting and delivering wood to heat the family's rural home. They also helped Betty with many financial decisions due to the loss of her husband's income.

A new county jail was under construction near where the family lived, and Betty was uncomfortable living so close to it. Several men in the congregation who were knowledgeable about real estate helped her find a comfortable and affordable home in town, on a street where she already knew her neighbors. This proved to be a wise move. The youth pastor began relating more intentionally to Jay.

A couple of years later, new pastors Kevin and Sharon Yoder arrived at Olive. They were impressed with how the congregation had responded to the Larson family. They soon recognized, however, that these informal efforts would not provide the long-term support the family would need. The two pastors studied the model outlined in the book *Supportive Care in the Congregation*. They learned that a neighboring congregation[8] had begun using a similar model, called Wraparound, with the help of a social worker from a community mental health center. The pastors attended a meeting to hear more about the Wraparound model and came away excited about the possibilities for their church. Wraparound uses an intensive, individualized case-management process with families who have serious or complex needs.[9]

Sharon and Kevin met with volunteers from the church who had been involved with the Larson family. They agreed to formalize their roles into intentional teams. Three separate teams eventually formed to offer ongoing support to the family. Kevin led the group supporting Betty. Sharon led the team for Jay. For a time, the pastors together led a family support group devoted to the needs of the daughters and other family members.

These teams have functioned as needed over the past seven years. Each team focuses on its own specific needs or concerns. As part of their pastoral roles, Kevin and Sharon have given leadership to the teams. Three persons with skills in finance serve as a subgroup to assist Betty with income, insurance, and other financial matters. After the youth pastor moved on to another setting, several young men initiated regular contact with Jay. They provide both emotional and social support. Jay is an active member of the congregation and plays on the coed church softball team. His support team is less formal than it once was, but relationships have remained strong as he interacts with his care group at church and other events. By now, others in the congregation fully include and affirm Jay's participation. They are always willing to help when asked.

Olive Mennonite Church support group. *Clockwise from left foreground:* Sam Brown (*dark shirt*), Nick Baughman, Kathy Baughman (*hidden*), Gary Miller, John Hahn, Jay Larson (*hidden*), Seth Haines, Jeff Mumaw, Maxine Yoder, Leroy Yoder, Betty Larson (*hidden*), Kevin Yoder, Norma Hahn, Angela Brown.

Betty's care group currently meets once every six weeks or so. Sometimes specific items are on the agenda, but the group remains flexible to changing the meeting's focus as needed. A crisis or other urgent matter receives attention as need arises. Betty cannot imagine what her life would have been like without the help of the support group over the years. She is most grateful for their help with decision making and finances. Both of her adult daughters now participate in her support group.

Members of the Olive congregation take seriously the Christian concept of being sisters and brothers to each other. One result of providing supportive care to the Larson family is that the initial support group members now find it easier to offer support to other members of the congregation when they have special needs. Supportive care groups in the congregation are a positive way of acting as an extended family to those in need. Support groups help identify needs and lessen problems.

At the same time, group members themselves feel blessed when they see God's presence in all areas of their work.

Pastors Kevin and Sharon acknowledge that the whole process has not always gone smoothly. They have used personal, professional, and other community resources, but much of what they have learned has come from "figuring it out as we go." They found that specific resources available did not always fit what the Larson family needed. Working with government bureaucracy has required perseverance and determination. Each breakthrough has added to their knowledge bank and helped them become even more effective in their supportive care of congregational members.

Jay has now completed high school and works in a local grocery store. He remains strongly connected to the church, where he is catcher for the softball team, plays golf, and manages the church basketball team. He enjoys meeting with a congregational mentor several times a month.

Betty is looking forward to becoming a grandmother soon and has a nursery prepared for when the little one comes to visit.

• • • • • • • • • • • •

Olive Mennonite Church is a small, diverse rural congregation with 150 years of history. What key elements make this support model work for them?

1. Over the years, the congregation has built a culture of sensitivity and attention to the needs of others. Church life includes the development of small groups and friendships beyond Sunday morning worship.
2. Supportive care for one family did not become an isolated situation. There are now at least two other care groups in place, responding to other needs in the congregation.

3. The pastors strongly support this model and play an active role in ensuring its success.

4. The Larson family is not only active in their congregation, but have also been active participants in the work of their own support teams.

5. Members have overcome their fear of offering assistance, while fully recognizing that they cannot solve every problem. They have learned the beauty of holding others up by walking alongside them and lightening their load.

3

Support for Parents

Pleasant View Mennonite Church and the Smith Family

When Ben Smith was a child, his laugh and smile were infectious. He enjoyed rooting for the Chicago Cubs baseball team, or pretending to be the next Michael Jordan with curly red hair. Ben was not a demanding child and was usually satisfied with simple ways to complete the task at hand. Ben would take time to "smell the roses," because for him every moment of life was meant to be experienced.

As a young man, however, Ben began hearing voices. He was eventually diagnosed with schizophrenia. Fortunately, he was part of a strong, loving family that looked for as many ways to support him as possible. Over the years, Ben's parents, Jim and Phyllis Smith, experienced much heartbreak and many crises while remaining highly committed and involved with their son. Although Ben was getting professional help from the local community mental health center, his parents found themselves struggling to know how best to support him.

While volunteering one day for the Anabaptist Disabilities Network, Ben's mother, Phyllis, discovered the book *Supportive Care in the Congregation* in the organization's resource collection. As she began reading, she felt a spark of excitement. This book might be exactly what their family needed! Phyllis and Jim reached out to Pleasant View Mennonite Church, their

The Smith family. *Left to right:* Phyllis, Ben, Jim (*seated*), Caleb, Josh.

home congregation in Goshen, Indiana. They approached their pastor, asking if he would help them form a group that could support them on their complicated journey with their son. He agreed, and together they began planning how such a group could come about.

The first step was educating the congregation about mental illness, schizophrenia, and Ben's particular needs. The parents first told their story to a small group they had been meeting with regularly for fellowship and prayer. Over several months, they widened the circle, sharing their story with five different adult Sunday school classes. Their efforts culminated in a Sunday evening program where they shared their family story with the whole congregation and invited those who felt God's leading to join their care network.

One care group volunteer said that listening to the parents speak from the heart inspired him to participate. "The parents shared openly with the church about their situation, and that can be so hard to do," he observed. "What motivates me has to do with what we promise each other when we bring new members into the church. We make a commitment to care for each other. We have a responsibility to help."

With the help of Jim and Phyllis, the support group established basic goals for their initial involvement with Ben. These included:

- Do something to improve Ben's housing.
- Invite Ben out to eat from time to time or to do other activities of his choosing to provide him with social interaction.
- Fill in for the parents when they needed to travel for Jim's work. (Support needs included reminding Ben to take his medication; taking him frozen, ready-to-heat meals; and helping him purchase groceries and clean his apartment.)

Due to Ben's limited disability income, he was living in an old, rundown apartment building. The property owner did not maintain the apartments, and the roof leaked. The building's elevator was broken, which meant that Ben's father Jim, who uses a wheelchair, could not visit him. The support group

Members of the Smith family's support team in 2007. *Left to right:* Bruce Sellers, Caleb Smith, Marilee Diener, Richard Christner, Richard Christner, Ralph Hartman, Phyllis Smith, Clay Shetler.

held cleaning parties several times a year to do deep cleaning. Eventually a local nonprofit housing corporation purchased the building. Following a complete building renovation, Ben was able to become one of the first tenants in the newly refurbished building. A brand-new elevator allowed Jim to visit his son in his own apartment for the first time.

The support group of ten people has been meeting regularly for nearly eight years. One of the members serves as the leader/facilitator for the group. Beyond that, organization is loose, with various people taking on specific responsibilities as needs arise. The group has occasionally assisted Ben with finding employment, health advocacy, and managing finances. However, Ben has not needed ongoing support in these areas. One member did help Ben find a job, which he worked for several months.

Ben does not participate in the support group himself because he does not like being with small groups of people or in large crowds. His discomfort with groups also keeps him from going to church and participating in a variety of other activities. The support group is still exploring how to provide ways for Ben to experience worship and foster his spiritual development. The group also continues to look for settings that might provide positive social interactions for him.

Ben knows everyone in the support group and trusts them because they are all friends of his parents. He communicates frequently with his parents, and is quite dependent on them for emotional and practical support. Because of that, it is critical that the support group be available to provide a similar level of support when his parents are out of town. Most group members have shown that they are strongly committed to supporting Ben and his parents in any way possible. They say readily that they will do anything they can to make life better for Ben and his parents.

The saying "a burden shared is a burden divided" aptly describes the benefits of such a support group. Reflecting on the value of the support group for herself, Phyllis says, "It is so comforting to know that I can lean on our support group by calling any member any time I have a problem or concern about Ben and they will offer help or at least caring support. After all, they have a history with our family and understand the issues."

Support group members agree that this experience has been mutually beneficial for all involved. One member put it this way: "This care group has become a support group for all of us. We experience God's presence as we discern Ben's needs as well as our own." When asked why he continues with the group, another member replied, "It has been a joy to stick with it. Knowing that you make a difference in another person's life brings encouragement in my own life. We have gained friendships, greater understanding of mental illness, a broader view of the church's mission, and the feeling that we're being the hands and feet of God."

· · · · · · · · · · · ·

What ingredients have helped Pleasant View Mennonite Church respond positively to this family and successfully establish and maintain a supportive care group?

1. The parents were willing to make themselves vulnerable and share their family story with their church.
2. The support group kept its goals small and manageable. Assignments taken on by individuals in the group were likewise limited.
3. The support group takes its cues from the family and maintains a strong sensitivity to Ben's desires and needs.
4. The congregation as a whole has a strong sense of mission and commitment to one another.

4

Advocacy and Support

Berkey Avenue Mennonite Fellowship and the Baker Family

Raising a family of five children can be a large task. Add to this the presence of special needs in some of the children, and the task becomes daunting. Doug and Cindy Baker arrived in Goshen, Indiana, twenty years ago with their five children and made Berkey Avenue Mennonite Fellowship their home church.

The Bakers had lived in an intentional community before moving to Goshen. Cindy was surprised to find intentional support within the Berkey congregation, too, even though its members do not live together in a typical intentional community. Among the factors that attracted them to Berkey was that the congregation already included several adoptive families who were dealing with children with challenges. Four of the five Baker children were adopted, and three were teenagers when they joined Berkey.

Cindy has appreciated the congregation's close-knit character. As members become aware of needs, they address them. Since they currently have no formal structure for supportive care, small groups play an important part in congregational

Cindy Warner Baker with youth and sponsors from Berkey Avenue Mennonite Fellowship. *Front row, left to right:* Seth Krabill, Corine Graber Alvarez, Cindy Warner Baker. *Second row:* Aaron Krabill, Mary Roth, Aaron Stiffney, Alisha Snyder, Emily Grimes. *Third row:* Trish Yoder, Lynelle Yoder Hofer. *Standing:* James Yoder, Andrew Shenk, Andi Born, Twila Albrecht.

life. Cindy and Doug relied frequently on their small group and others within the congregation as a circle of care. For example, one week when the Bakers accompanied the church youth group to Chicago, three different congregation families cared for their children. Having a strong small group network made this possible.

Through Cindy's advocacy work with the Christian Education Commission, the congregation has chosen to focus on the inclusion of persons with special needs in Sunday school. Cindy and Doug have been long-term youth leaders. They currently have an assistant whose role is to coach each youth with special needs toward integration into the class and to help other youth understand their challenges and needs.

Because of their own family's experiences, Cindy and Doug often find that other parents confide their struggles to them. The two often talk to the congregation's youth groups about the gifts and needs of individuals with special needs. Cindy says, "Understanding the strengths and needs of all of us encourages each to grow and become more of who God wants us to be."

Though the congregation does not have a formal supportive care network, important care work happens at Berkey Avenue.

As Cindy's children grew older, a network of church members continued to help them. Forms of support have included taking children to doctors' appointments, checking in when parents were out of town, coordinating transportation, and being available in emergencies. Support grew out of trust and a long-term commitment built over the years.

It has not always been clear how to address needs that arise in the congregation. For example, over a period of five years, Cindy and Doug had no choice but to take turns going to congregational meals because of their son's difficulty being in such overstimulating large-group settings. Other challenges have included finding ways to incorporate older adults with intellectual challenges into church life and integrating children and young persons with intellectual disabilities into existing Sunday school classes.

Cindy appreciates the downside of not having a formalized support system. It means parents need to advocate for themselves and their children, often during times when they are most vulnerable. Help with the small things gets lost in the shuffle. At times, parents carry too great a burden without the kinds of support that would be helpful to them. Berkey Avenue is just beginning a conversation about how to work strategically toward providing intentional support. Currently a special needs committee addresses needs, from adjusting to a new baby to dealing with chronic illness.

An intentional program would allow members to be more proactive and aware of needs. In the last year, responsibility for congregational care has expanded to include deacon care groups. Deacons check in with the individuals in their assigned group, keeping track of needs. Having a group of persons tuned in to needs is an important part of supportive care.

"When I'm receiving support from others in the church, they are representing God to me," Cindy says. "They express acceptance and generosity in a way that is very affirming and helps me to know that other people love and affirm my children and love and affirm me as a parent." She continues, "It can be demoralizing to ask for help when one of our children is in trouble. But grace has been extended to us regardless of choices our children have made, and our spiritual gifts have been affirmed."

Cindy provides support to others because of all she has learned from her own experiences. She also passes on this gift to others. She understands that even though parents may appear to be functioning well, a closer look might reveal that someone is really struggling. She continues to lead the congregation toward a more formalized structure for care and support, and to increase awareness and sensitivity for families and individuals who struggle with life on a daily basis.

. . . .

Berkey Avenue Mennonite Church does not yet have a formal supportive care network. So how did they reach out in support to families?

1. They used existing small groups to provide critical support.
2. The church affirmed Cindy and Doug's leadership gifts within the congregation to bring awareness to the needs of struggling families.
3. By exploring an integrated, comprehensive approach, the congregation stands a better chance of addressing a wide spectrum of needs.

5

The Business of Support

Chad Friesen was a keen observer of the world around him, even as a child. His family lived for five years in Jerusalem and Lebanon, which profoundly affected his worldview. As he grew older, this became evident in his artwork. His grade one teacher was the first to notice his artistic talent. His parents encouraged him to use art to express his feelings and make observations. Thus began his journey to become an accomplished artist. But the journey was not without barriers.

Alongside his artistic gift, Chad was experiencing unusual physical symptoms, which became increasingly debilitating as time went by. In 1976, when the family returned to the United States from an overseas assignment with Mennonite Central Committee, it became evident that Chad was suffering from serious health problems. He was becoming shaky when he walked and had experienced some convulsions. As he continued to lose muscle coordination, it became necessary for him to use a wheelchair to get around, especially in school. Even after Chad saw numerous doctors and specialists, a diagnosis

47

remained elusive. One doctor advised the family, "It's time to quit thinking about finding a diagnosis. Let's concentrate on getting him as independent as possible." With Chad's ataxia (loss of fine and gross motor control), it became increasingly difficult and frustrating for him to move toward greater independence.

In 1980, the family moved to Elkhart, Indiana, where Chad entered high school at nearby Bethany Christian School. An outgoing person, Chad made friends quickly. At home, however, he began feeling isolated. With his ataxia, he could not turn on the television or use a telephone. One way to increase Chad's independence at home was to purchase a micro-deck control center. This environmental control system would allow Chad to operate light switches, television, radio, telephone, and other electronic equipment by activating two sensitive switches that would respond to a light touch of his hands or feet. To help raise the $2,000-plus needed to purchase the control center, the family decided to approach groups in the community where the family was now involved. Chad's fellow students, along with his church, raised enough money to purchase the micro-deck control center and to install a ramp at his home.

This success provided Chad and his family with a greater degree of independence.

Chad's interest in artistic expression remained strong. To paint, Chad would lie on his stomach, prop himself up on his elbows, and steady his shaky painting hand with his other hand. Over time, this became more difficult and physically taxing for Chad. The paintings were stacking up, however, waiting for an appreciative audience.

Chad Friesen works on a painting.

His mother, Carol, a nurse, became his strongest advocate, ensuring that his medical, emotional, and physical needs were being met. She was not as sure how to help him develop the artistic dimension of his life. Painting can be an expensive hobby if you do not sell any of your artwork. His paintings needed a market, but he wasn't able to market them himself. In addition, the older he grew, the more his physical limitations infringed on his independence.

When Chad and his parents, brother, and sister first moved to Elkhart, they had joined Southside Fellowship, a congregation now part of Mennonite Church USA. From its beginning in the 1960s, this congregation had seen its mission as reaching out to those in need, promoting justice, and providing a supportive community for its members. Members often challenged one another to live out this mission actively. It was therefore no surprise when a pastor invited the congregation to support a member with disabilities in a unique way.

In 1990, Willard Roth, pastor at Southside, encouraged members to find a way to assist Chad. "Those of us close to Chad are aware he has the potential to use his gifts in an economically beneficial way. Chad is enriching us in very significant ways. He is a gift," Roth told the congregation.

As a church, we had questions. Could the church become an art broker and put on exhibits? Is that what the church should be doing? Those who had seen Chad's work had come to appreciate his unique style and use of bright colors to express feelings and frustrations, along with his spiritual, moral, and justice convictions. As Chad's speech became increasingly difficult to understand, his painting also became his communication vehicle—his diary, as he called it. God had given him a vocation; he had to paint. The church now considered the opportunity to help him live out his call.

A small group of individuals from our church became known as the Art Committee. They began meeting in the fall of 1990, with Chad and his mother, Carol, to explore how the church could be involved in helpful ways. I (Dean Preheim-Bartel) was part of that initial group from Southside. As a disabilities consultant with Mennonite Central Committee, I had known Chad's parents, Carol and LeRoy, before they moved to Elkhart. Now I was learning to know Chad, and we became friends. The Art Committee met many times over the next fifteen months to explore various ideas of assisting and supporting Chad. Finally we came up with a proposal and business plan. The committee recommended a business model to support Chad's long-term needs and goals. After a careful review by lawyers, accountants, and the congregation, the model received approval.

The business proposal required creating an independent for-profit corporation. Its for-profit status would prevent any possible conflict with the church's charitable status. The corporation would not interfere with Chad's eligibility for government disability benefits, which were essential to cover his healthcare and housing costs. The congregation would have no current or future financial obligations to the proposed corporation. It was also important to the Art Committee to view this venture as a business, rather than a charity to support Chad. At Chad's suggestion, we called the business God's Eye Art, Inc. Why? "In the Old City of Jerusalem," Chad recalled, "they painted the symbol of a God's eye above the entrances and gates. Seeing that eye reassured me of God's presence in my life."[10] The imagery stuck with Chad, and virtually all of his paintings included a God's eye.

To capitalize the business, family members, friends, and members of Southside purchased fifty shares at $100 each. Southside members made up 51 percent of the shareholders. The sale of shares generated a start-up fund of $5,000. Ownership of the corporation now rested with the shareholders, who in turn elected the board of directors and corporate officers, comprised of Southside members including Chad and his mother, Carol. Several of the six original board members served continuously for most of the twenty years the corporation existed. God had endowed each board member with unique skills and gifts: business and financial management,

Shareholders meeting, God's Eye Art, Inc. *Counterclockwise from far left:* Chad Friesen (*back to camera*), Carol Nickel, Dean Preheim-Bartel, Dierra Lehman, Merritt Lehman, Alton Longenecker, Willard Roth, Lois Longenecker, Sharryl Friesen, LeRoy Friesen, Shirley Souder.

organization and administration, creativity, woodworking, and flexibility. The group was an excellent match for the task. I had the privilege of serving as board president for fourteen years.

The board was a hands-on, hardworking board, serving without pay. Their primary responsibilities included marketing Chad's art; arranging for, selecting, and pricing paintings for exhibit; setting up exhibits; facilitating staffing of those exhibits; purchasing Chad's art supplies; and framing paintings for exhibit and sale. In addition, the board arranged for a series of art tutors to work with Chad to strengthen his artistic skills. From time to time, the board also served as a support and advocacy group for Chad and his mother as they worked through issues related to his care, living arrangements, and other personal needs.

Chad was an active partner in the business, and he let us know if he felt we were not taking his input seriously. On rare occasions, we would have artistic differences over his subject matter, composition, choice of colors, or framing (he liked fancy frames); but in the end his wishes as the artist usually won out. Christmas cards were always popular. We prodded him each July and August for new Advent paintings to be made into cards. He would complain, "How am I to get inspired in summer to paint about Christmas? If you can find me a real poinsettia plant in August, I'll paint it."

After we had decided to add a line of Christmas and greeting cards based on Chad's paintings, the board, along with other volunteers from the church, manufactured the cards in a garage. It was not yet financially feasible to have them commercially produced. Eventually, as technology advanced and production costs came down, we were able to have the cards printed by a commercial printer. The same company also made prints of Chad's more popular paintings, adding to the product line.

The board developed an organic style of working, not especially efficient, but critical for maintaining Chad's voice as part of a balanced decision-making process. Members developed a high degree of trust for each other's views and opinions. From time to time, we would go to the congregation and request volunteers to help staff exhibits and sell Christmas and greeting cards for Chad. The quick and joyful response indicated the congregation's commitment to Chad and his success as an artist.

A potter artist from our congregation hosted the first show of Chad's artwork, sponsored by God's Eye Art, Inc., in his studio/retail shop. The congregation hosted the second, open to the public, at our church. More shows and exhibits followed at a variety of venues. Around the holidays, our congregation frequently sold Chad's Christmas cards during fellowship hour. We obtained permission to do the same in other churches.

Annual shareholder meetings reported on the corporation's activities and presented financial statements. Shareholders knew when they purchased shares that they should not expect annual dividends. The board could choose to issue dividends whenever they felt there was enough net income. Shareholders also knew at the outset that they might never receive a return on their investment.

This model of support for an artist with physical disabilities proved successful in that the sale of paintings and cards generated enough income to maintain cash flow for the business and meet its overall objectives. It provided the art supplies Chad needed, plus a monthly stipend for him. During its twenty-year existence, the business grossed over $115,000 from the sale of cards, prints, and paintings. The board put on nearly a hundred exhibits and shows of Chad's artwork and sold an estimated five to six hundred paintings and thousands of Christmas and other greeting cards.

By 2008, Chad's health had deteriorated to the point that he was no longer able to paint. An art tutor who had been working with Chad for a number of years had the idea of producing collaborative artworks using clay, so together they created a series of creative clay masks. Chad would describe what he wanted the mask to look like, along with the colors to use,

Chad Friesen's painting *Circle of Love* was the inspiration for this book's title. The God's Eye, prominent in the upper right corner, appears in nearly all of Chad's paintings. His painting *The Crowds Following Jesus* appears on this book's cover.

while the tutor became his hands. Ultimately, even this activity became too difficult. Chad now needed almost twenty-four-hour medical care. To get the care he needed, he moved into a small group home for medically fragile adults in a nearby community.

The board continued to host exhibits for several years, but without new paintings, sales diminished. By late 2011, the board of God's Eye Art, Inc., decided to dissolve the corporation, since Chad was no longer able to produce new art. To reduce the remaining inventory of original artwork further, during November and December the board opened a gallery at the Old Bag Factory, a collection of art and specialty shops housed in a repurposed factory building in nearby Goshen. Over the twenty years between 1991 and 2011, Chad had produced an estimated eight hundred to a thousand paintings, and all but about 150 have been sold.

Chad died on November 15, 2013, at the age of forty-six. At his memorial service, an invitation went out to his friends to bring a favorite painting of Chad's for a final tribute to a man who truly lived his life to the glory of God. In his eulogy I said, "He often referred to his paintings as his diary—reflecting a full range of emotions, personal convictions, and his daily struggles with life. However, Chad was not one to dwell on 'what ifs' or 'why.' To the contrary, his paintings exude a passion for life, hope, even in the dark places (as symbolized by the God's Eye in his paintings) and a deep longing for justice in the world."

• • • • • • • • • • • •

What made this model work successfully for Chad and Southside Fellowship?

1. The idea of structured long-term support for a member was a good match with the congregation's mission.

2. The volunteers (board members) were willing to make open-ended commitments with somewhat fluid job descriptions for their roles.
3. The congregation was fully committed to supporting this venture and its success for Chad. Success was not dependent on pastoral staff but rather on lay leadership.
4. The willingness of church members, friends, and family to invest their time and money in this venture made success more likely. Their "skin in the game" kept them interested in the process and its outcomes.
5. Chad had a large and active hand in his own destiny. The rest of the people involved were always clear that everything they did ultimately had to benefit Chad or they should not do it.

6

Support for a New Mother

Oakton Church of the Brethren and the Wuhrman Family

Expecting a first child is an exciting time for any new parent. Make that twins and the potential for excitement more than doubles. Although she was carrying twins, Christine Wuhrman's pregnancy proceeded without problems. At thirty-seven weeks, she gave birth by Caesarean section. Bobby was a healthy boy, but his twin sister, Joanna, had serious problems. Medical staff whisked her away to the special care nursery, and her mother was not able to see her for twenty-four hours. Christine soon went home with Bobby, but Joanna was unable to leave the hospital. It took three months in the neonatal intensive care unit before Joanna improved enough finally to come home.

When the baby first arrived at home, she could not suck or swallow from a bottle, or breast-feed. She had to be fed through a nasal gastrostomy tube. At two months, surgeons placed a g-tube in her abdomen, which, five years later, still supplies most of her nutrition. The first months were difficult and included many emergency trips back to the hospital. Christine's mother, sister, cousins, and aunts all pitched in to help this fledgling family get through each week. Members of

Christine's church, Oakton Church of the Brethren in Vienna, Virginia, brought in meals, drove Christine and Joanna to the hospital, and provided childcare.

One member of the Oakton congregation felt the church could do more to support this family. With Christine in mind, she started an informal weekly Bible study and fellowship lunch group for stay-at-home mothers from the congregation. Although Christine was the only mother in the group who had a child with disabilities, these mothers quickly bonded and became strong supports for each other.

Two and a half years later, baby brother Ben joined the Wuhrman twins. Several months after Ben was born, the family went through a particularly rough time. The seizures Joanna had experienced from time to time since birth were mushrooming out of control. She began to have status epilepticus seizures, a life-threatening condition in which the seizure continues on and on unless arrested through medical intervention. In three months' time, her parents called 911 six times. Three of those times, Joanna was airlifted to Johns Hopkins Hospital in Baltimore. About a year later, she had three more hospital stays for gastrointestinal problems.

The family especially needed help during these various hospitalizations. At these times, the family received an outpouring of assistance and support from the mothers' Bible study group, Oakton's pastor, and other church members. They showed their support with extra prayer, childcare, meals, and letters of support.

From the beginning, the main purpose of the mothers' group was to offer fellowship and support to participants. When asked to comment on what the mothers' Bible study support group meant to her, Christine offered these reflections:

> I was excited about the formation of this group because, after having twins, I found myself feeling very isolated at home, and I was happy to have a regular connection to people. During the most difficult times, I sometimes felt disconnected from God, so the care group gave me the human connection I

The Wuhrman family. *Left to right:* Bobby, Christine, Joanna, Robert, Ben.

needed to make a bridge to my God. During the darkest times with Joanna, we had to confront the possibility of losing her. We were quite numb for several months after the crisis finally passed. When I would be sitting in the hospital for those endless hours with my precious little girl, I was so grateful to have my care group. I kept them informed with many emails and they knew just how to respond. They knew they were a part of the inner circle of support, and I deeply appreciated having them there with me.

The wider community in which this family lives is fortunate to have access to a variety of services for families of children with disabilities. Christine has taken advantage of these, including respite care twice a month and a monthly community support group for mothers of children with special needs.

Fast-forward another two and a half years. Joanna is now a petite, beautiful five-year-old girl with pretty blue eyes and thick, dark hair cut in a bouncy bob. Like all children, she fusses when she is sad, tired, or bored; she laughs and smiles when she is happy. When she is feeling good, she entertains herself and likes to clap her hands a lot.

Joanna shows significant developmental delays and communicates, without speech, through gesture and body language. She is learning to crawl. She uses standers and walkers both at school and at home to help her get around. Diet and medication now control her seizures well. Her gastrointestinal issues are always a big concern, but her parents try to stay on top of them. With Joanna and Bobby both in kindergarten, Christine is considering going back to work to help cover the many extra medical expenses.

At church, Joanna is starting to attend her age-appropriate Sunday school class. The teacher is a dear friend who knows her well. During worship, Joanna often plays in the nursery, and several of the nursery volunteers are getting to know her and learning how to respond to her particular needs. Joanna is well known and loved by members in the Oakton congregation, all of whom, in one way or another, have helped to welcome her into the body of Christ.

• • • • • • • • • • • •

While Oakton Church of the Brethren did not develop a formal supportive care network, they still found various informal ways of supporting this family. How did they do it?

1. In this small congregation, just about everyone was part of this informal support system.

2. The mothers' support group provided critical spiritual and emotional support, elements that are sometimes overlooked.

3. As the child with special needs grew older, the church continued to include her in age-appropriate ways, which was another way of supporting the parents.

7

Informal Support

Assembly and Pilgrims Mennonite Churches and the Jantz Family

Like many eleven-year-old boys, Ethan Jantz is curious, loves music and computers, and enjoys being on the go. He wants to be engaged in activities that interest him. Ethan is a pretty happy guy. Soon after he was born, however, his parents, Melissa and Tim, observed that Ethan was unusually fussy and hard to calm. He had trouble nursing at first, and did not nap or sleep well. As weeks and months passed, Melissa and Tim grew concerned about developmental delays. Melissa was increasingly exhausted with Ethan's care. It was especially difficult not having either Melissa's or Tim's parents or other family members nearby for support.

As a middle school teacher, Melissa loved children and had always hoped to have her own someday. She and Tim were excited when Ethan, their first child, was born. However, adjustment to motherhood did not come easily for Melissa, and caring for Ethan was taking a physical and emotional toll on her. She took a maternity leave for the fall semester after Ethan was born. She found she missed the daily contact with other people and engagement in school activities. Suddenly, her life revolved around nursing, changing diapers, and surviving on little sleep, with a growing sense of isolation.

Ethan was not meeting a growing number of developmental milestones; each in turn raised more red flags for delayed development. After consulting with the family's pediatrician, Ethan was evaluated and accepted into a state-sponsored early intervention program called First Steps. For the first time, the parents began admitting to themselves that something was "wrong" with their beautiful boy. From First Steps they gained useful tools to work with Ethan's language delays and sensory integration issues. They began, however, to fear the worst—that he had autism.

By age three, Ethan received the feared diagnosis of autism spectrum disorder (ASD). Though this diagnosis was hard to accept, it was also helpful because now his parents at least had a better idea of what they were dealing with. Nevertheless, the future looked rather bleak. Where could they find support for their family?

Melissa says, "I kept telling myself it will get better as he gets older." She watched the neighbor girls across the street riding their bikes and playing happily outside while their mother would occasionally pop her head out of the door to check on them. Melissa told herself, "See, eventually Ethan will do that, too; I won't always be tethered to a chair, holding the baby all day. The best is yet to come." Melissa felt shame for not feeling the euphoria other new parents seemed to show. Finally, after a year of denial and fighting her own feelings, she had to admit to herself that she was suffering from depression and needed to get help. Both parents were understandably struggling to accept the reality that their son had autism.[11]

During this time, the family was attending Assembly Mennonite Church in Goshen, Indiana. They asked the congregation for an anointing service, at which time they shared the struggles they were facing. There was an immediate outpouring of support.

Following this service, one of their pastors, Heidi Siemens Rhodes, took a proactive step by introducing the congregation to Ethan and his challenges in a comprehensive and positive way. She placed a flyer in every church mailbox that described Ethan and suggested ways to relate to him. It provided pointers on how to interact with him, what things might upset him, and ways to include him in church. Together with Melissa, Pastor Heidi met with Sunday school teachers to see how Ethan could best be included in Sunday school.

Several individuals volunteered to be with Ethan during the worship service so that Tim and Melissa could participate without having to run after him. Because loud clapping noises startled and scared Ethan, the congregation adopted the form of applause used in the deaf community—hands raised in the air and fluttering back and forth.

Reflecting on their experience at Assembly, Melissa commented some years later, "We've experienced a lot of grace, love, and support for us as a family and acceptance of Ethan by friends, family, and our church community."

The search to meet Ethan's needs led the family to pull up roots in Indiana and move to Pennsylvania, where therapies were more readily available and where Melissa's family would be nearby. Melissa said later, "While the church community and our friend circle were amazing, we were facing obstacles with insurance to pay for Ethan's therapies. We knew that Pennsylvania had a state-sponsored program we could benefit from. It was hard to decide that our family needed more, but we made a leap of faith. And nothing could replace our missing family support due to distance."

After the move, they began looking for another church that would be as supportive as Assembly had been. They were pleasantly surprised to discover Pilgrims Mennonite Church, which was already home to a couple with a much older son with autism. Within their first months of attending Pilgrims, the church invited both couples to share their parenting experiences of special needs children in an evening forum. After this time of sharing, church leaders asked both couples what would be helpful in terms of support. Within weeks, people begin volunteering to assist the Jantz family in a variety of ways. Several offered to be with Ethan during worship, while another added pictures to a photo album that Assembly had made for Ethan when they moved. Now the album also included people from his new church.

Pilgrims Church also gave stipends to both couples to use for respite care so that each could have time away as a couple. These funds were available annually and included a matching grant from Everence, an Anabaptist fraternal benefit association, which recognized the toll parenting a special needs child takes on a marriage. This gift felt deeply supportive to the couples. Melissa says, "The church wanted me and Tim to know that they were supporting us in having time together away from Ethan. Many people also invited us to their homes, asking what would make it easier for Ethan to be able to join us and for us to be able to relax and have a good time."

This outpouring of support was humbling for Melissa and Tim. Melissa confessed, "It is hard sometimes to be on the receiving end, but what I have learned about the presence of God from this experience is that people need to give just as much as I may need to receive. So to accept graciously the gift of time, of help from others is just as important as being able to give. And in turn, it makes me want to participate and give back when I have a chance in whatever small way I can."

Despite Ethan's continued growth and the many things that his parents have come to love about him, their parenting journey is not without pain. They realize that they may not have some of the experiences other parents have with their children—college, marriage, grandchildren. Then there is the fear of the future. Who will care for Ethan when the parents are no longer able?

Before fear engulfs her, Melissa says,

> I have to root myself back to the present. The journey with Ethan is different. Some days we're okay with that, and other days it is hard and it hurts. But then I remind myself of all the many ways I have seen God's hope and grace in our church experiences since having Ethan. I'm grateful for the invitations

to share my story, I feel acceptance, I feel heard, I feel seen, and I feel love. It is an amazing experience to have people reach out and give those gifts for no apparent reason except that you are in need and they want to help. I can't really put it into words what it feels like, but it is humbling and it feels like a little piece of the grief I carry with me gets chipped away each time it happens. It is healing.

The move to Pennsylvania has been a positive one for the family. Ethan participates in therapeutic horseback riding and an autism support classroom at the local elementary school. He will most likely be moving up to the school for grades five and six next fall. He has received speech and occupational therapies, and he is a client of the Philhaven Center for Autism and Developmental Disabilities. He has shared his abilities in a variety of ways in church, including playing drums while marching in the Easter parade. He loves to blow out the candle at the end of the service and say hi to everyone on the microphone. He enjoys spending time with his adult friends who volunteer to be with him during the morning service. More recently, he began attending a multiage Sunday school class.

On Ethan's eleventh birthday, his mother posted the following on Facebook: "The journey since Ethan's birth hasn't been what we first imagined it would be and hasn't been without its share of struggles. But there is more love than we can express for this boy who has turned our world upside down."

• • • • • • • • • • • •

Both Assembly and Pilgrims Mennonite Churches offered concrete support to this family without forming a formal supportive care group. What actions did the family and churches take to meet some of the family's needs?

1. The family opened themselves up by telling their story, thus creating an opportunity to address the family's needs.

2. A pastor at Assembly Mennonite took responsibility for further educating the congregation.
3. Pilgrims Mennonite looked beyond their congregation for resources to help families with special needs children, which enabled them to offer respite care grants.
4. People in both congregations were open to getting involved and quick to volunteer, even without a formal support structure in place.

8

Support for the Unexpected

Iglesia Menonita Arca de Salvación and the Maldonado Family

Josue and Norma Maldonado were anticipating the birth of their third child, six years after their second daughter was born. They were settled comfortably in Fort Myers, Florida, having moved from their native Puerto Rico. They were attending church at Iglesia Menonita Arca de Salvación. One of the first people to welcome them was Ruth Diaz Mellote, who immediately became friends with Norma and would soon become even more significant in their lives.

Routine blood tests just weeks before the baby's birth hinted of possible developmental problems. After she was born, Nyleea had complications and needed to remain in the hospital for two weeks. Tests

Norma and Josue Maldonado.

showed she had trisomy 21, or Down syndrome. What a shock for her parents to receive this difficult news! Through tears, Norma began to ask God, "Why me?" The first night after Nyleea came home, Norma continued her debate with God. She awoke the next morning with a miraculous sense that her daughter was really a gift from God, and determined to discover how she could provide the best care for her. At the time, both Norma and her husband had full-time jobs. Even though it meant reducing their family income, they agreed that Norma would resign her job and become a full-time mom.

How would she begin to educate herself? While Nyleea was still in the hospital, Norma spotted a few books on Down syndrome, but she did not find reading them helpful at first. She tried connecting with the organization Band of Angels, but soon found that her best help came from searching the Internet. There she found blogs by mothers with similar needs and a southwest Florida Down syndrome Facebook group. Norma is bilingual in English and Spanish, and through diligent research found resources in both languages. Help from her husband and two older daughters made her job at home easier. They continued their usual pattern of taking rest breaks together as a family. This reduced Norma's need for downtime for herself, but when she needed help, Ruth, her best friend from church, stepped in. Ruth's attentive care soon made her the primary person Norma trusted to care for Nyleea.

Ruth Diaz Mellote (*left*) and Nyleea Maldonado.

Nyleea progressed well physically and walked at thirteen months. Norma took care to have her checked regularly, while still avoiding the full reality of her daughter's delayed development. When her daughter was a year old, the family doctor suggested that Nyleea would be eligible for Supplemental Security Income and Medicaid. Though Norma was reluctant at first to admit that Nyleea's needs were this serious, the doctor convinced her that the programs would be beneficial. This word from a trusted expert helped Norma accept the extent of Nyleea's disability.

All along the way, David and Madeline Maldonado (no relation), copastors of Iglesia Menonita Arca de Salvación, found ways for the congregation to journey with this young child and her family. One Sunday, Pastor David arranged for Norma to share her testimony. He encouraged her to dream with the congregation about how they could offer even more support for families with disabilities in the church.

Norma began by sharing her vision for the church to start a nonprofit organization called See Me. The organization would provide for the social needs of children with Down syndrome and other disabilities. She also called for the church and the community to be inclusive in new ways. Further, she suggested that the church conduct educational sessions for the congregation. The sessions would teach children and adults, in age-appropriate ways, how to understand particular disabilities and relate to people with those disabilities. In response, the pastors gave the green light to See Me and are working to develop it as a ministry within the congregation.

Meanwhile, Nyleea has found her place in Sunday school. Despite her slight speech impediment, the music director has welcomed her as a member of the children's choir. On the third Friday of the month, the congregation holds a special children's service, in which Nyleea is able to participate fully.

Nyleea successfully completed public school kindergarten, but began having more difficulties in first and second grade, even with multiple Individualized Educational Plans. School difficulties led Norma to decide to homeschool Nyleea, beginning in third grade. Nyleea lives with the blessings of security and the love of a wonderful mother. Her mother finds blessing in the help of her immediate family and close friend, Ruth.

They all are grateful for being part of a loving congregation that is coming to understand what it means to be inclusive of people of all abilities.

While she has been busy caring for Nyleea in recent years, Norma makes time to give back to her church. She recently completed studies with Instituto Bíblico Anabautista (Anabaptist Biblical Institute), graduating from its on-location Christian leadership training program. She now serves as director of the congregation's Sunday school program for all ages, where she works to ensure that children of all abilities are able to learn and grow in their faith.

• • • • • • • • • • • •

What actions did the family and church take to meet some of the family's needs?

1. The family took time to grieve their daughter's limitations, but soon came to realize that she was a blessing. They committed themselves to learning how to provide the best care in a loving environment.
2. The pastors provided encouragement to the parents while working with the congregation to educate themselves on Down syndrome and intellectual disability; these efforts led to the formation of a new congregational ministry.
3. The person who initially welcomed them to the congregation became a loyal and trusted friend, who could provide respite care as needed.

9

Lifelong Support

Reba Place Fellowship and Bob Lembke

When Bob Lembke entered high school in his small town in North Dakota, he looked forward to the typical teen experiences of playing sports, making friends, and enjoying increased independence. During his first year, however, his life turned upside down. That year Bob noticed increasing muscle weakness and had a biopsy done. Doctors eventually diagnosed him with muscular dystrophy, a degenerative disease marked by loss of fine and gross motor control and a gradual loss of independence.

A few years later, when Bob was in his twenties, friends told him about Reba Place Fellowship, a Christian intentional community in Evanston, Illinois, just north of Chicago. Bob was intrigued and went for a visit in 1973. Four years later, he moved to the community. After several years of experiencing community life, in 1978 he made the commitment to join as a member.

When Bob first arrived at Reba Place, he was able to walk. A few years later, he began using a three-wheeled scooter to get around. He moved into a large household known as The Clearing, with about eleven other adults. One vital function of this household was to host guests who were coming to see if Reba Place was right for them. With Bob's gift of hospitality, he adapted easily to his new environment. He especially enjoyed listening to guests' stories.

Reba Place Fellowship is unique. According to the community's website, the group formed in 1957 "as an alternative Christian community where all things are held in common." The community has close ties to Reba Place Church, a Mennonite congregation that evolved from Reba Place Fellowship in the 1980s. The Fellowship's website describes the faith and values that hold the group together:

> The meaning of our lives is not found in the pursuit of individual happiness, in personal careers or accumulating possessions according to the American dream. Rather, Jesus invites us to a shared life defined by his call to "love one another as I have loved you." This love has the power to transform ordinary human beings into gifted members of the Body of Christ—a whole new way of living together in mutual service and forgiveness that is good news to the world now, and the beginning of eternal life with God.

> Participants discern together how to best work for the common good and make decisions about their lives together in community, all through Spirit-led consensus. They also share times of celebration and mourning, times of thanksgiving and lament. Their common bonds, rooted in the person and life of Jesus give meaning to the joys and sorrows they share as part of God's work to redeem the world. For them the body of Christ is a very practical reality. The Christian life was meant to be lived together.

> Participants of Reba Place Fellowship seek to fulfill their mission and the mission of Jesus by being a community of love and discipleship. . . . They feel that alone, none can fulfill this mission, but committed to one another as the body of Christ, they are given God's Spirit to do God's work.[12]

These expressions of the community's faith and life have been central to Bob's faith. While living at Reba Place for the past thirty-seven years, Bob has participated fully in the life of the community and, as much as possible, in the household chores. In recent years, his condition has declined to the point where he requires around-the-clock care. Over the years, his household has stepped in to provide the progressive level of care he has needed. Community life has spared him the frequent changes in staff that many people with disabilities reluctantly accept.

Julius Belser, one of the founding members of The Clearing household, became Bob's first care provider. Julius, inventive with handyman skills, often created assistive devices to help Bob live more independently. At first, Julius helped Bob get up in the morning and get ready for bed at night. As Bob's needs increased, other men in the household took over these roles. Bob worked at the local high school in the library, where he received some assistance from the staff. After his job at the high school ended, Julius was on call to help Bob during the day. As Julius grew older and Bob's needs increased, the group needed to find someone else to provide full-time care and service coordination. Julius discerned that David Hovde would be the best person for this role, and invited him to become Bob's caregiver.

David already knew Bob well, having come to live in the household seventeen years earlier. Several years after moving to Reba Place, David had become part of the L'Arche Communities, finding meaningful work assisting people with developmental disabilities and building community with them. When Bob Lembke needed a new coordinator of care, David seemed to be the logical choice. David now sees that in some ways he had been preparing for this call for a long time. David had left L'Arche and had been living at The Clearing again for more than seven years, so he and Bob were already friends. For David, the community's call to be Bob's care partner was the next step in God's plan for his life.

On the Fellowship's website, David shares his story, recalling the faith journey that brought him to Reba Place:

> Something was lacking in my life: a strong faith in God's love for me. I poured out my soul to God in prayer, expressing

longings, requests, and confessions, but still lacked a strong sense of God's care. I became interested in reading about the Holy Spirit in the Bible, and other books, and talking with others about it. I had hope that in learning more about this I might find a deeper sense of God's love. Another missing piece in my life was the opportunity to use my gifts to meaningfully contribute to society. Then I discovered Reba Place, and on my first visit I found hope. I remember the particular moment my spirits lifted. After a meal a household member talked with me, listened to my struggles and said he felt God might be calling me to Reba Place.

David moved to The Clearing in 1994. As he reflects back to that time, he readily describes the decision as one of the most important he has ever made.

After my arrival, I basked in the mealtimes and common work. I learned how to cook much better. I attended church worship and meetings. Participating in heartfelt singing, dance, and other expressions of worship moved me to tears. I witnessed others communicating in the Holy Spirit, and believed that I also could hear the Holy Spirit in me. My prayers no longer seemed to float out into space without receiving any response. This place has truly become home for me. It's been a place where I've discerned what kind of work God calls me to. It's been a place of faithful friendship. I've also had painful trials but I've known God's spirit with me through them all.

David has been responsible for coordinating Bob's care for the past three years. His daily routine includes getting Bob up and dressed in the morning, feeding him at some meals, and assisting him with other personal care during the day. Another man in the household, Michael Killian, helps Bob to bed at night. Carl Sherrod, who also lives at The Clearing, is on call with a monitor in his room to help Bob during the night. Others are available to assist as needed.

Reba Place members never consider *if* they will provide care needed by one of their own; the question is only *how* they will provide it. This is how they live out their commitment to

Left to right: David Hovde, Bob Lembke, and author Linda Christophel at The Clearing.

be present for one another's needs, no matter what they are, up to and including full-time assistance such as Bob requires. Providing this kind of hands-on support and assistance from within The Clearing household has meant that Bob can live surrounded by the friends and community he loves, and not need to move into a nursing home or other institution.

Bob receives government financial assistance that pays for his caregiving. David is employed forty hours a week through a homecare agency and receives pay from them. This makes it possible for David to devote himself full time to Bob and not seek outside employment.

Bob eats his meals with the household, meets many guests who pass through, and contributes spiritually, if not physically, to the household. David makes it possible for Bob to participate in the intentional community practices, such as weekly small and large group meetings and annual retreats. The two of them also attend an annual camp with Joni and Friends, a Christian retreat specifically for families that include members with disabilities. This time away is special and offers a variety of

activities, encouragement, care, spiritual support, and understanding of the challenges of life with a disability.

Sharing in prayer in small group settings is especially meaningful for Bob. Several years ago, someone suggested to David
that he and Bob read the lectionary readings together. David
says, "This has been such a blessing for both of us. I experience God's presence through these times of reading, sharing,
and praying together with Bob. I experience God's presence
through my relationship and friendship with Bob. As a fellow
community member, housemate, and friend, I feel called to do
this. I have purposeful work in being a care partner with Bob."

• • • • • • • • • • • •

For most church congregations, taking responsibility for the
level of care needed by Bob may seem overwhelming or imprac-
tical. So what made it possible for Reba Place Community to
provide this kind of care all these years?

1. Intensive supportive care is part of the "DNA" of
   this Christian intentional community. Their energy is
   focused on *how*, not *if*.
2. At Reba Place, getting to know one another intimately
   over time reduces the anxiety of providing personal
   care to members, should that become necessary.
3. Inviting someone to take on a supportive care role may
   be just as important for the caregiver as it is for the
   recipient of that care. Those who are gifted and called
   by God to be caregivers should not be denied that
   opportunity.

Other Models of Congregational Support

As we searched for stories of congregations practicing the values expressed in *Supportive Care in the Congregation*, we heard about congregations that communicate care in a variety of ways. This final chapter shares glimpses of several more congregations that support the day-to-day lives of members or neighbors who live with disabilities. These churches use a variety of support models, some more enduring than others. What is notable is that in every case the church responded positively and compassionately to a need they spotted. This happens only when families or individuals feel safe and become vulnerable enough to share their story and identify their particular needs.

College Community Mennonite Brethren Church

Sometimes individuals with a disability become pioneers in their own congregation. Linda Martens is one of these pioneers. When Linda was born in 1964, few opportunities were

Members of the College Community Mennonite Brethren Church
Friendship Class participate in communion. *Left to right:* Linda Martens,
Mark Wiens, Kevin Smith, Julie Lewis.

available to children with severe disabilities. As a preschooler,
she experienced developmental delays and numerous medical
issues. Her parents, Wilfred and Erma Martens, were concerned about what was happening to their daughter.

With her parents, Linda attended College Community
Mennonite Brethren Church in Clovis, California. As a child,
she attended Sunday school with the other children of her congregation. By the time she reached age twenty, however, the
church seemed to have no place for her. Her parents began
meeting with others in the congregation with similar concerns.
In 1990, they formed the Friendship Sunday school class.
Initially the class had two students, a young man and Linda,
but it soon began to attract persons from outside the congregation. Thus began, thanks to Linda, an outreach ministry of
this church.

As followers of believers baptism, the congregation was in
favor of baptizing a young adult with intellectual disabilities,

and a few members approached Linda's parents suggesting the possibility of baptism for her. A small group representing the congregation met with her parents and concluded that Linda was ready. The pastor met with Linda and developed a simple set of questions to which she could respond in professing her faith. The pastor also modified the way in which the ordinance (sacrament) would be performed. Mennonite Brethren churches typically practice baptism by immersion, but in this case the pastor and Linda walked into the baptistery. He poured the water of baptism on her head instead of immersing her. Once again, Linda had been a pioneer in her own congregation, thanks to the relationship the congregation already had with her.

In the early 1990s, congregational restructuring included the creation of a new Supportive Care Commission charged with ministry to persons with developmental delays and their families within the congregation and in the community. Laypersons run the ministry, but the pastor plays a critical role in welcoming people with disabilities and providing support in times of crisis. Linda's parents were instrumental in shaping this commission. It continues to be a vital ministry today.

When Linda was in her late thirties, Wilfred and Erma became concerned about how she would receive care in the future. Arrangements were made with Central California Residential Services to set up a staffed apartment in a nearby facility where Linda could live. She was excited to move into her own place. The Supportive Care Commission from church arranged for a housewarming and provided monetary gifts for her future needs. Linda's move allowed Wilfred and Erma to plan for their retirement years.

What happened in their congregation has been an answer to prayer for Wilfred and Erma Martens, lifelong advocates for their daughter and others with disabilities in the community. Their dream of a church where people with disabilities are an integral part of congregational life has been realized.

Akron Mennonite Church

Some years ago, Akron Mennonite Church in Akron, Pennsylvania, began forming ministry teams to address particular needs in the congregation. About this time, Phil Rutt and his family were planning to take their adopted daughter, Elizabeth, back to see her birth home in Vietnam. The Rutts' twenty-four-year-old son, Philip, however, was born with multiple disabilities, including cerebral palsy and blindness. He needed around-the-clock care and could not make the trip.

With the help of close family and friends, a ministry team of six persons formed to care for Philip during his parents' trip. Team members trained to care for Philip's needs stayed with him in shifts during the entire time his family was gone. Following the Rutts' return, the team remained active, providing ongoing relationships for Philip, as well as additional times of respite the family.

Nelson and Esther Hostetter, an Akron Mennonite couple, took steps to form a supportive care group for their son, Chris, as they prepared to move to a retirement community. Chris lives with a variety of disabilities due to a congenital neurological condition. While he was living independently and had a part-time job, he still depended on his family and others for daily living supports and transportation.

Nelson and Esther wrote a letter to friends of Chris asking if they would commit to being a support group for him. Many of these friends were already relating to Chris in significant ways and agreed to form an informal support network. The parents hoped that if the friends knew about others who were also involved with Chris, they would be more willing to lend their support. Most, but not all, of these friends were from Akron Mennonite Church, and most responded positively to the letter. Nelson and Esther have continued to explore ways to improve connections between these persons (some of whom did not previously know each other) and with Chris.

Holdeman Mennonite Church

Because of professionally trained members within the congregation, Holdeman Mennonite Church of Wakarusa, Indiana, has adapted the secular model called Wraparound to provide supportive care to persons in their congregation with particular needs. When members ask for help, or when their need becomes apparent, pastors invite them to choose persons for a Wraparound group that will support them. Trust is central to this selection process. Group members come from different walks of life and bring their own perspectives and life experiences to this support role. Groups meet about once every three weeks, or more frequently in times of crisis.

A professional therapist from the congregation leads the Wraparound group. In group meetings, the person receiving support shares what is going well in their life and the challenges they are facing. Group members ask questions for clarification. The group provides ample affirmation for the person struggling with a particular issue. They may also challenge the individual concerning decision making, rationalizations, or options to consider.

The church has used this model to provide supportive care to numerous individuals over the years. Prayer support, Christian love, and caring support are valued additions to the Wraparound model as the church implements it.

The Basilica of Saint Mary

Support for many everyday aspects of life is what the Basilica of Saint Mary seeks to provide to its worshiping community and neighbors in Minneapolis, Minnesota, on a large scale. This large congregation's broad approach contrasts with the person-by-person approach typical of smaller congregations described in this book. The Basilica is a place of worship, refuge, and peace for nearly 6,700 families. On its website, the Basilica describes itself as a gathering place for people of all faiths and races. It is a center for the arts, and a place of refuge for the poor. It sees itself as a community committed to the growth and social well being of the city where it serves. The Basilica provides supportive care through ministries that assist with employment, new shoes and boots, Meals on Wheels, mental health, grief, disability awareness, life skills and mentoring, and struggling families stabilizing their lives.

The church's employment ministry provides one-on-one assistance to individuals seeking employment. When the person seeking assistance has a disability, a member of the Basilica disability awareness committee works with them more intensively. This person helps the employer understand ways to accommodate the individual. A member of the awareness committee may provide ongoing support on the job until the person is well established. This committee also focuses on educating the congregation about various disabilities and helping to reduce barriers that individuals with disabilities might experience in their church participation.

The Basilica's mental health ministry includes education and awareness in the congregation and providing resources and support to individuals in need. Because of its prominent location, people with serious mental illness come to the Basilica for help on a daily basis. The mental health committee actively provides support to those who come for assistance. Some of those who have received assistance have gone on to volunteer for the Basilica. As they share gifts for the benefit of others, friendships grow, and the staff is able to assist with any needs that emerge.

Seattle Mennonite Church

God's Li'l Acre is a drop-in center for people experiencing homelessness in the Lake City area of Seattle. Seattle Mennonite Church established the center several years ago as an outreach ministry. Individuals who come to the center are typically suffering from the effects of post-traumatic stress disorder, bipolar disorder, schizophrenia, alcoholism, substance abuse, domestic violence, poverty, or physical ailments resulting in disability.

Volunteers run God's Li'l Acre with oversight from a member of the pastoral team. Volunteers and staff receive training in offering person-centered, trauma-informed, recovery-oriented companionship. The ultimate purpose is to extend hospitality in the context of community to people experiencing homelessness.

The center offers showers, laundry facilities, personal storage, and other basic survival needs for people living on the street. God's Li'l Acre also connects people with a wide range of community resources through the neighborhood's task force on homelessness.

God's Li'l Acre volunteers emphasize that they receive a great blessing by participating in this ministry. While offering friendship and support to their guests, the volunteers receive much more in return. One volunteer reported that he saw God's hope and grace at work daily, from the sharing of a meal and conversation around the table to the giving of material gifts. "Just being present with people whose pain is different from our own is the greatest gift God has ever blessed me with," he comments. The program's director adds, "Hope is believing that every person is created by God uniquely and gifted, and that dignity is often shrouded by the experience of suffering, illness, and addiction. Being in a space where people are reminded of who they are in the eyes of God is healing and hope filled."

Epilogue

What do you take away from these stories? If you are a parent, perhaps you find renewed determination to share your story and not to be afraid to ask for what you need. If you are a person with a disability, perhaps you take courage to be your own advocate. If you are a pastor, perhaps you resolve to offer yourself as a guide to fearful people. If you are a congregation member, perhaps you accept the challenge to enter into mutually enriching relationships with others who experience life differently. If you are a friend, resolve to act now by challenging what you think you know, and determining to make a difference in the life of another. Your hour to act has come.

Acts of compassion need not be grand, but can begin with the smallest of gestures by reaching out to another person in times of stress, disappointment, or loss of what might have been. A touch, a tear, a hug may be the best prayer you can offer. Everyone deserves to be treated with dignity and seen as a child of God, created in God's image.

Henri Nouwen says it well: "A Christian community is . . . a healing community not because wounds are cured and pains are alleviated, but because wounds and pains become openings or occasions for a new vision. Mutual confession then becomes a mutual deepening of hope, and sharing weakness becomes a reminder to one and all of the coming strength."[13]

Each of these is a story of hope: hope for a better future, hope for restored dignity. And hope that we all can be open to new relationships, new experiences, and courage to move out of our comfort zones. May we be transformed by hope until with all humility we can say, as did a volunteer from Seattle, "Just being present with people whose pain is different from my own is the greatest gift God has ever blessed me with."

Notes

1. Gregory Boyle, "A Conversation with Greg Boyle (Reading Group Guide)," in *Tattoos on the Heart* (Simon and Schuster, 2011), http://books.simon andschuster.com/Tattoos-on-the-Heart/Gregory-Boyle/9781439153154/reading_group_guide, accessed March 3, 2015.
2. In reference to the vision statement of Mennonite Church USA entitled "Vision: Healing and Hope": "God calls us to be followers of Jesus Christ and, by the power of the Holy Spirit, to grow as communities of grace, joy and peace, so that God's healing and hope flow through us to the world."
3. Evelyn Gunden, "Church Uses Kent's Gifts," Mennonite Central Committee, *Dialogue on Disabilities* 7, no. 1 (Winter 1986), 1–3.
4. Robert Baker, "Kent a Part of Belmont," *Mirror Reflections from the Mennonite Disabilities Committee* 1, no. 1 (December 1987), 1–2.
5. Dean A. Preheim-Bartel, Aldred H. Neufeldt, Paul D. Leichty, and Christine J. Guth, *Supportive Care in the Congregation: Providing a Congregational Network of Care for Persons with Significant Disabilities*, rev. ed. (Harrisonburg, VA: Mennonite Publishing Network,

2011). Available from MennoMedia and other online booksellers.

6. Duane Beck, "Just Tell Them," *Mirror Reflections from the Mennonite Disabilities Committee* 1, no. 1 (December 1987), 1–3, 4.

7. At their request, we have used fictionalized names for the "Larson" family members.

8. Holdeman Mennonite Church in Wakarusa, Indiana, described in chapter 10.

9. National Wraparound Initiative, Portland State University, http://nwi.pdx.edu/, accessed January 30, 2015.

10. Roberta Carpenter, "Local Painter Remains Undeterred by Disability," *Goshen News*, May 26, 2002.

11. Quotes in this paragraph are from Melissa Jantz, "Reflections on Motherhood," *The Femonite* (blog), August 13, 2014, www.femonite.com/2014/08/13/melissa-jantz-reflections-on-motherhood/, accessed January 26, 2015.

12. Reba Place Fellowship, "Our Life Together," www.rebaplacefellowship.org, accessed January 31, 2015.

13. Henri J. M. Nouwen, *The Wounded Healer: Ministry in Contemporary Society* (New York: Doubleday and Company, 1972), 96.

Recommended Resources and Contact Information

Recommended Resources

An extensive annotated bibliography of resources selected for those interested in developing a congregational supportive care network is available in *Supportive Care in the Congregation*, listed below.

Preheim-Bartel, Dean A., Aldred H. Neufeldt, Paul D. Leichty, and Christine J. Guth. *Supportive Care in the Congregation: Providing a Congregational Network of Care for Persons with Significant Disabilities.* Mennonite Publishing Network, 2011. Order from MennoMedia, www.mennomedia.org, 1-800-245-7894.

Ruth-Heffelbower, Duane. *After We're Gone: A Christian Perspective on Estate and Life Planning for Families that Include a Dependent Member with a Disability.* Mennonite Publishing Network, 2011. Order from MennoMedia, www.mennomedia.org, 1-800-245-7894.

Contact Information for Churches and Organizations

Akron Mennonite Church
1311 Diamond Street
Akron, PA 17501
717-859-1488
www.akronmench.org

Anabaptist Disabilities Network
3145 Benham Avenue, Suite 5
Elkhart, IN 46517
574-343-1362
www.adnetonline.org

Assembly Mennonite Church
1201 S 11th Street
Goshen, IN 46526
574-534-4190
www.assemblymennonite.org

Basilica of Saint Mary
P.O. Box 50010
Minneapolis, MN 55405-0010
612-333-1381
www.mary.org

Belmont Mennonite Church
925 Oxford Street
Elkhart, IN 46516
574-293-5160

Berkey Avenue Mennonite Fellowship
2509 Berkey Avenue
Goshen, IN 46526
574-534-2398
www.berkeyavenue.org

College Community Mennonite Brethren Church
2529 Willow Avenue
Clovis, CA 93612
559-291-3344
www.clovismb.org

Holdeman Mennonite Church
65723 CR 1
Wakarusa, IN 46573
574-862-4751
www.holdemanmc.org

Iglesia Menonita Arca de Salvación
3629 Michigan Avenue
Fort Myers, FL 33916
239-561-3993

National Wraparound Initiative
www.nwi.pdx.edu

Oakton Church of the Brethren
10025 Courthouse Road
Vienna, VA 22181-6018
703-281-4411
www.oaktonbrethren.org

Olive Mennonite Church
61081 CR 3
Elkhart, IN 46517
574-293-2320
www.olivemc.org

Pilgrims Mennonite Church
21 S 12th Street
Akron, PA 17501
717-859-2986
www.pilgrimsmennonitechurch.org

Pleasant View Mennonite Church
58529 CR 23
Goshen, IN 46528
574-533-2872
www.mypv.org

Reba Place Church
535 Custer Avenue
Evanston, IL 60202-2920
847-869-0660
www.rebaplacechurch.org

Reba Place Fellowship
737 B Reba Place
Evanston, IL 60202
847-328-606
www.rebaplacefellowship.org

Seattle Mennonite Church
3120 NE 125th Street
Seattle, WA 98125-4515
206-361-4630
www.seattlemennonite.org

Southside Fellowship
140 W Mishawaka Road
Elkhart, IN 46517-2223
574-293-2825
www.ssfelkhart.org

Authors

Dean A. Preheim-Bartel spent his career as an administrator in social service and church-related agencies, including director of Mennonite Developmental Disabilities Services. He specialized in developing programs and building coalitions. In his retirement, he is working in his gardens, doing landscape design for others, and spending time in his wood shop. He is currently learning more about disabling conditions, as he lives with Parkinson's disease.

Timothy J. Burkholder devoted most of his working years to church relations at congregational, conference, and denominational levels. He recently served two years as executive director of the Anabaptist Disabilities Network. After retiring, he contributed volunteer time to this book project. He and his wife, Sharon Burkholder, have three adult children and two grandchildren.

Linda A. Christophel has worked as a social worker in the public school system for twenty-four years. In this role, she has worked as an advocate for students with disabilities and as a consultant to their families and to school staff who educate them. Outside work, she enjoys oral history, movies, travel, her backyard garden, and spending time with family and friends. She and her husband, Joe, have three adult children and two grandchildren.

Christine J. Guth has been working for the Anabaptist Disabilities Network since 2006 and currently serves as its program director. She is a graduate of Anabaptist Mennonite Biblical Seminary and a licensed minister of Mennonite Church USA. She helped to found a mental health recovery clubhouse and a support group for parents of children with autism in Goshen, Indiana. She and her husband, Robert Guth, have two adult children.

CPSIA information can be obtained
at www.ICGtesting.com
Printed in the USA
FFOW02n0134110617
36605FF